The Music Was Just Getting Good

the final poetic mixtape by

Alicia Cook

Andrews McMeel
PUBLISHING®

All that's left of what was—
amidst the dermis and dust—
is a ghost limb twinge of delight
and piles and piles
of these poems to grieve by.

Mostly written in Newark, New Jersey,
between March 2020 and April 2023

Dedicated to
Ryan, Logan, Jordan, Jaxson,
Isabella, and Liliana

Love,
Aunt Alicia

Also by Alicia Cook

Stuff I've Been Feeling Lately
I Hope My Voice Doesn't Skip
Sorry I Haven't Texted You Back

Life can be a lot.
This book can be too.

The Music Was Just Getting Good
covers sensitive, potentially triggering material.

Take breaks whenever you need.

Follow "thealiciacook" on Spotify and
listen to *The Music Was Just Getting Good*'s
OFFICIAL PLAYLIST!

"We've become bored with watching actors give us phony emotions. We are tired of pyrotechnics and special effects. While the world he inhabits is, in some respects, counterfeit, there's nothing fake about Truman himself. No scripts, no cue cards. **It isn't always Shakespeare, but it's genuine. It's a life.**"

—*The Truman Show*

SIDE A

The Poems

Track One

Maybe this year will be my year.

Maybe I'll start going to bed before midnight.
I'll stop sleeping through alarms and commit to
a morning routine. Maybe I'll start texting
people back more and RSVPing YES less
reluctantly. I'll stop counting calories and end a
three-decade-long war with the mirror. Maybe
I'll stop bringing knives to a gunfight. Maybe I'll
even stop showing up to the fight altogether.
Maybe I'll remember what day trash day is. I'll
buy a plant I need to water, grow my own mint,
and learn more about soil. I'll go to the dentist.
Maybe I won't hear from you and be okay with
that. Maybe I'll call it even.

Maybe this year will be my year.

Currently listening to:
"1999" by Prince

Track Two

I'm sorry I didn't get up with the dawn chorus.

I'm not sure if you've heard,
but outside we're at war with the elements.
There's burning and drowning all around,
so I went back to bed, clutching my weighted
blanket like a life vest.

No need to place your finger
beneath my nose or across my wrist.
I'm just good at playing dead;
good at judging when it's safe to come back out
again.

Every day is the same, isn't it?
The wrens and robins.
The dystopian catastrophes
streaming live from our screens.
Some refuse to accept what this means:
if the world is on fire, then so are we.

The emails hope they find me well,
but I'm too unwell to respond.
My mother hasn't heard from me in a week;
in her voicemails she reminds me to eat.

I've not been myself for so long,
I fear I've become someone else.
I inspect my hands. My fingerprints remain.
I am not really lost; I am somewhere still,
so that's something.

By all available metrics, I'm doing well,
but every time I stand up I'm dizzy.
By all available statistics, I'm not alone,
so that's something.

Currently listening to:
"Carry It Well" by Sam Fischer

Track Three

Some of my best friends
have moved away from me.
It's hard not to take growing up
and moving on personally.

Once upon a time, we were children
who jumped into piles of raked maple leaves
with our two front teeth missing
without the pull to analyze why
we found such joy
playing in heaps of dead things.

We've forgotten how to rest.
Or maybe the ability
was taken away from us
when we weren't looking.
Like a stolen superpower.
Like a mermaid's voice.

Peace has become a faraway pastime.
One that often feels beyond
the realm of possibility now
but we remember the simpler times
and how our innocence took them
for granted.

None of that was our fault.

Now, always gasping,
but we recall the full breaths—
the full stops—fondly.

Currently listening to:
"Nobody Tells You When You're Young"
by Andrew McMahon in the Wilderness

Track Four

I am not short and sweet.

I am a long mess of rambling knots; enough of an enigma to entice a closer look, pretty enough to convince you I am worth unraveling. You'll try to undo my tangles until your hands are scraped raw. Then you'll give up because you have nothing left. You will realize I'm actually made of bramble and barbed wire and not worth the scratches.

Listen to me.

I am not the clearing in the forest. I am the havoc and brush that keeps you lost. I am not clear water.

I am zero visibility, and you will drown.

Currently listening to:
"You Know I'm No Good" by Amy Winehouse

Track Five

In the blinks between
what was and what is
there is a room.
Those who have died
take a ticket, a seat, and wait.

They flip through photo albums filled with the
grins of everyone they ever loved.
They sip their favorite beverage and snack their
favorite snack.
(All complimentary, of course.)
Parting messages from the living blare over the
intercom and their most beloved memories play
on a loop across the screens suspended above
their head.
(Projected on 35mm film, no matter the decade.)
When they glimpse out the window,
it's their preferred time of year.

Then, their name is called—pronounced
correctly.

In the waiting room to the afterlife
deserving souls are given peace.
The last thing they see isn't unfamiliar or
jarring—not the face of hate or a shattered
windshield.
The last thing they feel isn't fright or pain—not
the grip of disease or strange and unusual
hands.

You see
in the waiting room to the afterlife,
deserving souls never die confused.
No matter how brutal, sudden,
lonely, or boring.
To them, it's always just like falling asleep.

Currently listening to:
"Wildflowers" by Tom Petty

Track Six

By the third missed call,
I'm convinced you're dead.

Hopefully warm in your bed
or in your car with your favorite song playing.

Dead anywhere but
the Rite Aid bathroom—
surrounded by strangers
more inconvenienced than heartbroken
upon finding your body.

Dying is a private pilgrimage.
            The nerve of you to carry it out in a
public space—
one I need to pass on a regular basis.

I'm forced to go about my day
Like you're not dead.
            How dare you.

Post office.
Pens are out of ink and the line is too long.
Plus, you're dead.

Gas station.
Attendant tells me I'd be prettier if I smiled.
Plus, you're dead.

I drive off. Doing the math—
fourteen hours since last contact.
There's no saving you by now.
You're cold. Probably blue.
Morticians have makeup that could help with
that.

What was your last thought?
Did you think of me?
You're my only thought these days.
I heard it's just like falling asleep.
Does that mean you'll still get to dream?

Tell me you at least had I.D. on you.
Make that part easy on us, please.
Because the rest of our lives
are going to be so hard.

The truck in front of me kicks up something.
The starburst the rock creates in my windshield
mimics the symmetry and sparkle of my
earrings I know you love.
You told me when you weren't dead.

I begin to bargain.

If you're not dead,
I'll give you the earrings.
          Even if you sell them.
          Even if you die in them next week.

At least we'll have another week.

Twenty-seven is such a cliché age to make an exit.
Just wait another month—
be an individual and die at twenty-eight instead.
I swear I—abruptly
          my phone buzzes.

It's you.
You're not dead.

Currently listening to:
"Soon You'll Get Better" by Taylor Swift (featuring The Chicks)

Track Seven

I am lying to you. Calling my manic behavior "productivity." Calling my depression "laziness." Calling my burnout "introversion." I'm slow to respond but fast to make up an excuse for the delay. I wrote a whole book about this before, so at least give me some credit for my consistency.

What would I say to you anyway? That my therapist told me to write down five reasons why I'm happy to be alive, but I could only think of four? (You were one of the four reasons.)

The noise from life just beyond my front step sounds too much like that piercing static from the Emergency Broadcast System test and not enough like music for me to venture out.

I realize that every time I'm even remotely tired of living, there's always something to remind me why I'm alive.

Maybe that's my fifth reason. *There's always something.*

Currently listening to:
"Noah (Stand Still)" by Noah Cyrus

Track Eight

The Whisper:

I never got into your favorite music. This frustrated you. You used to whisper, "You have to let your ear adjust. Then you'll see."

The Scream:

I never became your favorite song. This saddened me. I used to scream, "You have to let your heart adjust. Then you'll see."

Currently listening to:
"LAX" by Conor Oberst (featuring Phoebe Bridgers)

Track Nine

It's like we forget how hard December can be on our hearts.

On our patience. On our minds. And each year when this final month rolls back around, we create these lofty goals and pack our calendars and smile really big in pictures. But then the sky stays gray, and we have trouble getting out of bed. Trouble getting into the shower. Trouble finding parking. Just trouble, trouble, trouble. Some call these feelings of despair and burnout the "holiday blues," but it's depression. December is often a wolf dressed in sheep's clothing for many. Our preexisting struggles are compounded by the pressure to be our best selves just because it's supposed to be the most wonderful time of year. Well, December's impossible expectations of humankind could crush anyone, even those who appear to have every reason in the world to celebrate.

Oh, difficult December, please take it easy on us.

Currently listening to:
"December" by Sara Bareilles

Track Ten

I'm pulling pine needles out of a pocket of a jacket I haven't worn in over a year / they're brittle but still sharp / a lot like my heart these days / one pricks my finger just enough to draw a wince / and a perfect circle of blood / it's been so long since I've felt jolly / or social / or alive / but gifts still need to be wrapped / I still need to show up / *I'll be whole for Christmas / if only in my dreams.*

Currently listening to:
"Home for Christmas" by Everly

Track Eleven

I am murk and mud. You are clear eyes and blue
skies. I throw phones out of apartment windows
and scream until my throat embers catch fire.
You are not used to those things. You are used
to punctuality and people calling back when
they say they will.

I'll never make sense to you because we are not
the same. Because your mind is clear and kind
to you. Because silver linings find you naturally.
Because you fall asleep in two minutes flat and
wake up before your alarm. Because you've
never embarked on an apology tour or have
written "I'm sorry" inside of a birthday card.
Because when you swing open your front door,
you see sapphire skies, while I see the
apocalypse. And that doom is as real to me as
those sweet fluffy clouds are to you.

You tried with me. You handed me peace of
mind, but I didn't know what to do with it. I
expected it to singe, so I flinched—let it slip
through my fingers and shatter at my feet. I
stepped over the pieces and went on with my
life. You stayed and swept up the mess.

I abandoned myself like a failed rescue mission.
Let the flashlights go dark. Let the thoughts and
prayers dwindle. Accepted being yesterday's
news. I didn't just need space away from myself,
I needed years. You kept searching. You never
lost the plot in all of this.

I never thanked you for walking through the ankle-high snow to get me a hot pretzel that one night. I never thanked you for cleaning the blender I left behind in the sink or for folding my clothes. I never thanked you for putting up three Christmas trees the year I believed I had nothing left to celebrate.

I owe you one.

Currently listening to:
"I Can't Love You Anymore" by Maren Morris

Track Twelve

I didn't know that snow globes contained more than just water until one shattered across the airport floor. The man who mopped it up muttered something about antifreeze. I looked it up and he was right. It was our second winter together and you kissed me as the baggage carousel kicked into gear. You tasted like warm airplane wine. We weren't paying attention to anything except one another so our bags spun past us. It was all fine. The broken snow globe. Your stale cabernet breath and glassy Jack Frost eyes. Having to wait longer for our bags. It was all fine.

Currently listening to:
"You and Me on the Rock" by Brandi Carlile

Track Thirteen

My mind always leaves situations before my body.

I know I am done long before I walk out front doors for the last time. For me, pain is easier to manage in pieces than all at once. I come to grips in a staggered fashion. Maybe that is why I never liked ripping bandages off as a kid. Even though my parents constantly explained that removing it in one swoop would actually hurt less than slowly pulling bit by bit, I took my time peeling them off my skinned knees; let them dangle from my body. I've always preferred resting between winces, instead of screaming all at once.

In delaying the inevitable, I prepare myself.

Currently listening to:
"Gone Girl" by Olivia O'Brien

Track Fourteen

We used to end our conversations by saying "I love you to death."

What I think we actually meant to say was "I love you through death," because when your heart stopped, mine started pumping twice as hard for the both of us. "I love you through death," because all these years later we have nothing in common but our last name and the short days we spent together and the love I continue to carry.

"I love you through death," because there are some types of connective tissue that can never be broken down by time.

Currently listening to:
"That's How Strong My Love Is" by Otis Redding

Track Fifteen

Cowritten with Christopher Andrews

Winter is here;
frost across my skin.
Thaw the paintbrush,
color me bruised.
Navy, Baby, Indigo too.
Shades of blue
for each cold snap
between me and you.

The streetlights pop at 4 o'clock
and I'm supposed to let you go.

I don't want to be in love
with anyone else.
Can you make room for me?
Can you do this soon, for me?

Spring came and went,
but the showers didn't relent.
Petals pressed between words I never said.
Rehearsed my dramatic,
cinematic exit from you
but I never found my moment;
and I always missed my cue.

The streetlights pop at 7 o'clock
and I'm supposed to let you go.

I don't want to be in love
with anyone else.
Can you make room for me?
Can you do this soon, for me?

Summer stumbled in
just the way you always did.
You kissed my mouth,
and said, "It's getting cold out."
You could taste it—
the ending on my tongue.
I learned what I deserve
so you'll never be the one.

Now the streetlights pop at 9 o'clock
and it's time to let you go.

Currently listening to:
"Never No More" by Aaliyah

Track Sixteen

All hail the hypervigilant heir!

Older sister, worried about
the wayward one in the middle
ever since we were little.

Made of glass, placed on autopilot because
people around me required a lot of maintenance.

Doubtful. Depressed. Curious. Careful.
Went to bed hoping others would wake up the
next day.

Family praised it as "independence,"
employers labeled it "autonomy,"
someone else once called it "lonely."

Born with too old a soul and
diagnosed with a chronic case of empathy.
I've forgiven everyone I've ever met
but can't forgive myself.

I flinch a lot when you drive
because I never trusted anyone with my life.
And now you know why.

Currently listening to:
"Surface Pressure" by Jessica Darrow, from Disney's Encanto

Track Seventeen

This story is based on an unreliable narrator's internal monologue.

Sorry if my blinks appear impatient, but you're twenty seconds into your story and I already worked out how it ends. I am bored but also polite so I don't talk over you. The car that pulls up next to us at the rest stop has snow on top of its roof. I wonder where they are coming from. This month has been warmer than the trees appeared, at least back home. As in, the leaves had long since fallen but the ocean wasn't cold to the touch yet. There is a chaotic buzzing in my head; I'm a fly caught behind blinds in the bathroom. The hand dryer never dries my hands enough, so I go back into the stall for some toilet paper. I mention my inner monologue to you once we are back on the road and you have no idea what I am talking about—you don't hear your voice in your head all day long. You can't relate. We arrive and I wonder when the hotel covered the outdoor pool and if the firepits are already set up and when—then you say aloud, "I love the quiet. There's just something about the off season."

Currently listening to:
"WHY" by NF

Track Eighteen

I didn't want to miss a day, but things got in the
way. I wanted to spin straw into gold. Wanted
to call you back. Wanted to sing along with you
in the car. Wanted to fill up your cup so badly
that I poured from my own. Wanted to sustain
the unsustainable. Wanted full speed ahead.
Wanted to have something to talk about over
tacos. I wanted to press my body into
champagne powder and create the most
beautiful snow angel you've ever seen, elevation
be damned. But when I laid down on the
ground, I fell asleep.

It is tiring being someone to everyone.
Who am I, to me?

Currently listening to:
"(still) not your hero" by Highland Kites

Track Nineteen

A cold front is sweeping across the East Coast,
but not where you are.
Remember that night I slipped on the ice
hidden in plain sight getting into your car?

You laughed.

The bruise on my thigh
lasted for over a week.
The pain woke me up
each time I rolled over
in my sleep.

There were never enough pillows
on that bed.
I always woke up
with a stiff neck.

You sure took a lot of pictures of me
for someone who never planned on staying.
You never worked out your own shit;
I stayed until I was humiliated, regardless.

But last joke's on you
because when my fever finally broke,
the whole house shook.

Losing you was not for the fainthearted.
I felt like I had put out a yearslong wildfire
I'd been gaslit into believing I started.
I should have known,
all those nights waiting alone.

Dinner always got a little cold.

Currently listening to:
"Merry Nothin" by Jesse Reyez

Track Twenty

Even soft-landing goodbyes have left me
sad and lost and confused.
And each time, I didn't know what to do
except pray that time would do its job for once
and   fix   me.

Will I ever be at peace with myself?
Will I ever be able to sit still next to you?

That's not your question to ponder.
Not your ailment to remedy.

Don't take a slower look.
I am not a healthy sport to spectate.
Keep a neutral spine.
Don't invest too much faith in me,
my pendulum heart can sway either way—
at a moment's notice,
at a slight change in the tides.

Swim ahead. I will catch up.

Currently listening to:
"Mirror" by Kendrick Lamar

Track Twenty-One

We hugged goodbye. I think? I tell people we
did. I don't remember what type of sandwiches
we had for lunch that last day. I wore a white
shirt to your funeral. Maybe? My pants were
definitely a size too big. I know my sister
touched my shoulder in the church when I was
breaking down. Or was I already broken and
just no longer cared if anyone knew? I probably
figured they wouldn't notice in all this quiet
chaos. Your coffin was three inches away from
us, and everyone was trying to accept that, even
though your body was right there, you were
absolutely gone. Did they assume just because I
was alive, that I was fine? I knew . . . I knew I
could decompose right in front of their eyes and
they wouldn't see it. Years went by, actually,
and they still didn't see it . . . my breaking.

Currently listening to:
"F64" by Ed Sheeran

Track Twenty-Two

On easy days, you compare me to the Grand
Canyon on a beautiful afternoon. You say we
both take your breath away, make half-formed
words fall back into your throat. You say we
both swallow sound, create quiet peace in a
world of loud war.

On difficult days, you compare me to the Grand
Canyon at night.

This makes more sense to me.

Because you've only ever had limited visibility
of me. And each time you edge closer, you risk
falling to your death. The night sky over the
Canyon reveals long-dead stars and planets. My
night sky produces its own skeletons and
remoteness.

Nothing prepares you for the Grand Canyon in
the dark.

And nothing could have prepared you for me.

Currently listening to:
"Gramercy Park" by Alicia Keys

Track Twenty-Three

You stopped dreaming of peace treaties. You
stopped dreaming of pouring two inches of
fresh concrete over all of the fault lines and
punch lines. You stopped dreaming of the day
the wipers would keep up with the rain.

You've started to dream of making a break for it
in the most dramatic ways possible, so the
escape mechanisms won't jam.

You dream of forgetting to water the tree so the
Christmas lights burn the house down. You
dream of the broken home going into
foreclosure as visions of bulldozers dance in
your head. You dream of abandoning humidity
and booking a one-way ticket to the desert. You
dream not of the vengeful kind of vengeance,
but of the solace kind.

Currently listening to:
"Kill Bill" by SZA

Track Twenty-Four

I always feel an odd relief whenever I pass a funeral home and notice that its parking lot is empty.

No one in this particular neighborhood is sucking on stale mints while someone they love is breathless, sewn into the last dress they'll ever wear.

No one is watching themselves smile in a slideshow, a picture frame, or on a glossy poster board they found in Walgreens, while coming to grips with never being that person again.

No one is having any of those other eccentric, private thoughts in a public space that buzzes with the constant, low hum of elevator music and sporadic sobbing.

No one is wondering if they should walk around and greet people they only see when they have a dead person in common.

No one is wondering where they are going to put all those flowers or casseroles, since there isn't enough space in the house or refrigerator for all of that sorrow.

No one will have to keep a list of who sent what, to write thank-you notes later. *Thanks for acknowledging my person died with a fruit basket!*

No one needs to find where the extra light bulbs are hidden in the basement or decode passwords or worry about how many death certificates they should request.

No one needs to fear what tomorrow will be like, or the next day or the next.

That is because no one is here. The parking lot is empty. What a relief.

Currently listening to:
"Over the Rainbow" by Judy Garland

Track Twenty-Five

It is not always about getting through the day. It's about breathing through each individual moment. Some days, you open your eyes and say:

"Just step into the shower." / "Just lace up your sneakers so you get the fresh air and music and coffee you love." / "Just get to work so you can be distracted for eight hours."

When it gets really bad, and your hands never warm up enough to smile, it's about staying around for others.

"Return home, someone can't eat dinner without you." / "Go to sleep, someone needs your heart to beat next to theirs." / "Wake up, because there are people on this planet who need you to start another day beside them."

Currently listening to:
"Hope" by Ada Pasternak

Track Twenty-Six

I haven't been well since July's fireworks. I missed my window to get it together because now the temperature has turned against me and the sharp wind bites my face and it's dark when it shouldn't be. As far as my nervous system is concerned, I'll be in power-saving mode until we change the clocks again.

I'm the only one who can pull myself out of this slump but I keep putting it off. I'm going to come back from this. But right now, I'm just numb and unruddered. So I wait in front of the fireplace for a miracle. I know it's coming. The hard will soften again.

We misplace and regain joy much like that hour we lose or our fawn-like footing when we learn to ice-skate; we learn to fall safely, we learn to get back on our feet again.

Currently listening to:
"Good News" by Mac Miller

Track Twenty-Seven

Put down your pencil
I'm not testing you.
Put down your tools
I'm a heartbeat, not a machine.
Put down your knife
or I'll keep running into the blade.
Put down your guard
I'm not a threat to anyone but myself.
Put down your spotlight
I am not remarkable.

I am a human, hurting—
one who needs sleep, optimism, magic, support,
a break from the breaking.
All I need is for you to tell me you will love me
whether I get better or not.

Currently listening to:
"River" by Leon Bridges

Track Twenty-Eight

Sometimes someone else's world will come to a stop, and you'll feel it for a moment.

A rattle of a light. A tremble in the ground. A flash of déjà vu. A quiver of a lip. A draft through a concrete wall.

But then it passes, and you go on with your day. Annoyed with life and its tiny disturbances. Mad at your coworker. Late for dinner.

Because today you're the lucky one while someone else is sitting in a cold dark room with the nine circles of hell cracked open beneath them.

Currently listening to:
"Eyes on You" by Sara Bareilles

Track Twenty-Nine

The snow is better rested than I
this time of year.
It sleeps heavy upon the roof,
making its presence known occasionally
by groaning loudly above my head.

'TIS OUR SEASON!

You visit my mind's eye
like the Ghost of Christmas Past.
In this impatient hibernation, I wait
for the temperatures to transition
above what reminds me of you.
For what is dead to resurrect—
for the pipes to thaw and sing
for the grass to remind us that it is green.
It cannot stay this cold forever.

I know I've spent one day too many regressing
in our old town because I've started to fantasize
of a parallel universe.

One where I never defected from this place, and
you grew up in time to realize what we had
when we had it.

We are all susceptible to revising our memories.
My footsteps have developed a slower cadence;
nostalgia and regret, when mixed, tends to
thicken the atmosphere.

Now time zones and lifetimes apart,
six hours ahead of you isn't enough.
But just between us:
Merry Christmas.

Currently listening to:
"multiverse" by Maya Manuela (featuring PEMBROKE)

Track Thirty

How long can we remain steady? As long as it takes.

There is no safe zone in these circumstances, the floor is lava. We're forced to walk along tightropes as thin as filament but nowhere near as incandescent. Our hands, shaky. Our nerves, frayed. But our bones remain determined. This isn't the same balancing act we performed as children on the curbs in front of our houses. We are untrained and ill-prepared acrobats, but we're fast learners. And so, we continue our funambulist dance, because at least we are inching forward, dispelling the man-made myths of time and age and solid ground.

Eyes up.
Push back against the cold or
you'll catch your death.
Our voyage isn't over yet.

Currently listening to:
"Why Would I Stop?" by Big Sean

Track Thirty-One

Grief is like a yawn—contagious; involuntarily triggered when we see another person in mourning. We grieve their loss. We bury our dead all over again. We imagine loss we haven't lived through yet. What is both frustrating and comforting about the ripple effect of the grief wave is that it only happens because our hearts are linked. Tied to another and another and another. So, when one heart breaks, the reverberations strike the hearts of others. So, when one person dies, a little bit of everyone they ever touched dies alongside them.

Currently listening to:
"Bones in the Ocean" by The Longest Johns

Track Thirty-Two

I have always hated snow. A main topic of conversation during any first date. I felt like I should come clean about it right away. Before things progressed and the things like "cabin" or "Vail" or "do you ski?" were uttered.

I hate how snow encloses me, forces me to dig myself out of the grave I live inside. How it invokes nostalgia: pancakes and poached eggs and you and that apartment. How it reminds me of myself, pretty and pristine until touched and disturbed too much.

I must admit, snow and I share the same deceptive qualities! Like how you thought you could glide over my surface unscathed, only to be suddenly swallowed by a deep crevasse.

Currently listening to:
"Shittin' Me" by A$AP Rocky

Track Thirty-Three

Somewhere in the middle of nowhere
lies who you used to be.

Before your fortress burned down with you
inside. Before the fair-weather people left you
for dead. Before the scavengers ate up the
breadcrumbs that could lead you back.

Somewhere,
on the edge of what once was, you sleep—
unaware that you've started to let others
mispronounce your name
because if you are not sure who you are
anymore, how could they be?

There's a certain loneliness
that comes with self-preservation.
Deep inside your fun-house-mirror mind
remains a portal only you can access.
You can get there in life's pitch blackness,
without a map.
Without a yellow-brick road.
Without the second star to the right.
Without a time-obsessed rabbit.

You're at home in your elephant graveyard—
a place others can't manifest into existence
even though they've been by your side for years;
even though their shirts have collected your
tears.

This sacred place is not your final resting place,
but a place you can finally rest.

When your eyes drain hollow and lose focus,
and they shake you and ask, "Where did you
go?"

Well, now they know.

Currently listening to:
"Lion Witch Wardrobe" by Carly Moffa

Track Thirty-Four

I am not desensitized; I am burned out.

Overwhelmed again. Calling coffee a meal
again. Too tired to focus but too exhausted to
sleep again. Sitting down in the shower again.
Breaking out in hives again. Snapping at you
again. Apologizing to you again. Having weird
dreams again. Not believing in much again.
Crying on the trail or in my car or at
commercials again. Losing perspective again.
Feeling like the end of the world is at my
doorstep again.

You can shrug it off and say it's all in my head
(again). Even if that is true, I spend more time
here, in my head, than I do anywhere else on the
planet. Shouldn't my mind be a habitable space?
All this dense fog in the air should have lifted by
now.

Out in the distance a guiding beacon glows.

A deep orange takes the shape of hope.
            A lighthouse, maybe.
                    A sunrise, perhaps.

Currently listening to:
"There Is More Love Somewhere" by Bernice Johnson Reagon

Track Thirty-Five

I heard a new song, and I felt guilty.

I was bothered by my check engine light, and I felt guilty. I laughed at something really funny, and I felt guilty. A mosquito fed from me, a bee startled me, a bird landed next to me, and I felt guilty. I was drenched by sudden rain and was reminded how cold snow was after it snuck into my boot, and I felt guilty. I experienced phones getting smarter and things getting streamier, and I felt guilty. I watched my parents and pets age, and I felt guilty. I fell asleep under a weighted blanket, and I felt guilty. My nose freckled from the sun, the creases around my eyes dug deeper, and I felt guilty.

I kept growing older, and I felt guilty.

You died, and I survived, and I felt guilty.

Currently listening to:
"In The Stars" by Benson Boone

Track Thirty-Six

Forgive my self-exposure,
but I must admit that though I love my life,
I'm not always in love with my life.
It's not you, it's me.
Congestion collects.
Eyes become heavy.
Sighs become labored.
Dust accumulates inside of me,
dulling my stained-glass heart.
I clumsily keep existing,
losing and recovering hope and momentum just
like my serotonin.
Then, the sun cracks through the clouds when I
least expect it; the barren trees transform from
brown into gold.
And I am inspired, filled with the belief that I
can do the same.
At any moment, on any day.
I clean the tarnished prism within
and the rainbow returns.
I outgrow enemies and grudges.
I move beyond things I accept I can't move
and take time repairing my own crumbling
infrastructure instead.

Currently listening to:
"Days Like This" by Van Morrison

Track Thirty-Seven

You can't stay put anymore; you feel the blizzard brewing behind your eyes and need to get out of dodge. Starting over is a lot like falling through a soft spot of a frozen pond. You know the risk, but something compels you to get on the ice anyway. You're smiling, gliding—until the plummet, the gasp, the Cold Shock Response breathlessness of it all.

After the plunge comes the thawing process. You'll inspect yourself and may notice you have become broken under the frostbite. Your stem bent, your roots fractured. While tempting, don't romanticize the way the ice once encased you; it wasn't a makeshift cast that once was holding you together—it was keeping you numb. The ice wasn't protecting you from the elements—it was leaving behind its own burns.

Recovery is sometimes nonsensical. The warmth has returned, you are hurting. Realize that's a good thing. It means you're getting the feeling back to your heart, and the healing process can begin.

Currently listening to:
"I've Gotta Be Me" by Sammy Davis Jr.

Track Thirty-Eight

The basement door isn't the only thing in this house that has become unhinged.

I'm fine, until the next time. I spill water, and I cry. I watch a commercial, and I cry. An unexpected meeting gets added to my calendar, and I cry. I remember you're going to die one day, and I cry. My inner turmoil is starting to leak all over the place, and I am just too tired to clean it up. Does turmoil leave behind an inky stain? I hope not, I like our floors. Did I step into the chaos or am I chaotic? I've always been too close to myself to tell.

I reach compromises between myself and my brain, daily. To avoid throwing dishes against the wall, I decided I was just going to throw away all the mason jar lids. To avoid packing my bags, I just donated most of the clothes hanging in my closet.

You find these concessions peculiar because you have no way to know what almost happened instead. You don't know how bad it could have gotten.

Just the other day you laughed and nonchalantly said, "Hey, remember when you threw out all the mason jar lids?"

How can I forget? It was never about the mason jar lids.

Currently listening to:
"Gasoline" by HAIM

Track Thirty-Nine

You were born in a snowstorm
but died in a heatwave,
leaving me somewhere in the middle, holding
space for two resentments.

If grief had a smile,
it'd be the slope of a snow drift.
If grief had a war cry,
it would scorch one's lungs to ashes
and still demand we create sound.

Grief strikes suddenly
and pierces unforgivingly;
an icicle dropping like a knife
from right above my head,
hot pavement blistering my bare feet.

Currently listening to:
"Joanne" by Lady Gaga

Track Forty

You are endemic to my heart.
We met, and all the clocks went dead.

You slipped into me like silk;
energy percolated into my body.
I absorbed you like a nutrient,
became an active weather system.

I swear, lightning sparked from my fingertips.

We loved each other back when hot coffee was
still being served in styrofoam cups and my gas
gauge was broken so I had to keep track by
resetting my mileage. Back when I wore the
sequined dress that made me itch and we ate
lobster mac and cheese for the first time. Long
before I gave up alcohol and you found
psychedelics.

I used to fall asleep—phone in hand, ringer on;
I didn't want to ever miss your voice.
Now my phone has been on silent since 2016.

We wasted so many hours on one another,
back when we had time to kill.
Now minutes mean too much to me.

Currently listening to:
"Rest In Peace" by Dorothy

Track Forty-One

When some were still new enough to cry over
losing balloons to the sky, I was losing people.

I don't think you understand how that has
changed how I interact with the living.
Loneliness is a constant vibration just below my
surface. My thirst is unquenchable. There has
always been something a bit sad about me. Most
noticed in my eyes and in my choice of men. My
heart is always a little bit broken, even when I
am in love. Apologies are easier for me to accept
than compliments. Unbalanced scales become
pedestals because maybe I deserve the
compliments I am not accepting and maybe you
don't deserve the forgiveness you're taking. I'm
a disaster moonlighting as a New Jersey success
story; a beautiful view out of the window of a
train wreck.

Equal parts prodigy and project, the fixers
always become infatuated with me.

Currently listening to:
"Big Casino" by Jimmy Eat World

Track Forty-Two

I offered myself to you.
I felt your disappointment before I heard it.

"I have this already."

Your sigh as sharp as peppermint aftershave.
You knew how much I was worth, and you set
me aside in such a haphazard fashion.

You knew I was young enough to break.
Young enough to think my world was over,
just because you weren't in it.
Young enough to have to lie to my parents,
who had yet to uncover the eating disorder
but recognized you were making me sick.
Young enough to think if you couldn't love me,
no one would be capable.

Years later, you tell whoever will listen
that I am the one who got away.
Years later, I stop blaming myself,
saying, "What did I know? I was only a kid."

Currently listening to:
"Ghost" by Jack Ingram, Miranda Lambert, and Jon Randall

Track Forty-Three

I repressed my twenties like one bad memory.
Closure and peace aren't always mutually
exclusive.

I may not have totally settled up with my past,
but we often call momentary truces. My
melancholia has an open-door policy
as long as it doesn't overstay its welcome.

I may cry but I smile too
and sometimes my sister and I laugh so hard, a
different type of tears pool in our eyes.

And a handful of former classmates who made
my life miserable now keep up with me on the
Internet and invite me to their MLM events.

Youth was never my favorite experience,
so much of it felt unimportant.
I've always stood on the tips of my toes,
been the bigger person,
but I am still growing.
My stitches are still dissolving.
The glue is still drying.

I still yearn for the impossible
like a brain without the ache,
a heart without the pain.
Even though I know
it doesn't work that way.

I try to be as gentle as possible with myself,
as not to wake the sleeping giants.
It's a delicate situation, co-existing with these
monsters of my own creation.
I may not always feel great in my skin, in
harmony with my mind,
but I feel at home.
At long last.

Currently listening to:
"Could Have Been Me" by The Struts

Track Forty-Four

Any day we can get out of bed and go about our
normal lives is a good day. Our normal / hectic
/ exciting / mundane / momentous / difficult /
easy / happy / sad / frustrating / euphoric /
rainy / sunny lives filled with toothbrushes and
car keys and appointments and family and
movement and beautiful boredom that we will
miss one day.

Take a slower look,
life can change between blinks.
Take a softer look,
the ground can freeze overnight.

Currently listening to:
"Day After Tomorrow" by Phoebe Bridgers

Track Forty-Five

Trips down supermarket and chapel aisles. Trips over obstacles and words. Trips to hotel rooms and emergency rooms. Trips to ice cream parlors and funeral parlors. Trips to gas stations, banks, and piano lessons. Trips that see Christmas slide into New Year's, and sunsets transition into sunrises. Trips to the coast and to the mountains. Trips to see scattered friends who used to live around the block and family who used to live under the same roof. Trips with a window seat. Trips when you're stuck riding in the middle. Trips that arrive early. Trips that are delayed or canceled altogether. Trips to the maternity ward and nursing home. Trips to rehab. Trips to the vet and to the park and to the rainbow bridge. Trips to parent-teacher conferences and graduations. Trips to protests. Trips to concerts and movies and concession stands. Trips to kitchen tables and white-cloth restaurants and drive-thru windows. Trips to the dreadful side of a memory and trips to the good old days. Trips to the unknown that eventually twist into familiar roads. Trips to moments of nauseating boredom, unrelenting tears, uncontrollable laughter. Why yes, life is a trip. The best trip there is.

Currently listening to:
"A Little Bit of Everything" by Dawes

Track Forty-Six

When I first lost you, I was warned that grief
will startle me awake every day until, one day, it
won't. One day, I will sleep through the night
again. Then, I will find myself trying not to feel
sick over the lack of sickness. Guilt will enter the
room. I will get mad at myself the first time I
allow myself to laugh in front of your parents.
Then, something else will happen. Peace will
knock and I will answer. I will find a picture I
have never seen before. And I will smile and not
feel guilty. I will feel grateful. Grateful for the
picture. For you. For the time we did have.

Currently listening to:
"Hey, That's No Way to Say Goodbye" by Leonard Cohen

Track Forty-Seven

My father once told me there is an incandescent darkness inside of me and that he believes in reincarnation because his idiosyncrasies have been reborn through me more than he'd ever wish.

This doesn't worry him, though.

He explained that on this earth, one's internal fire either wreaks havoc or illuminates the way ahead. But, on rare occasions, a person possesses a hybrid of these flames.

"You're one of the special ones," he assured me. "Because you can appreciate the start and the end of things, and find a certain relief in both."

Currently listening to:
"Growing Sideways" by Noah Kahan

Track Forty-Eight

Cowritten with Carly Moffa

I wasn't keeping secrets
you just didn't ask the right questions.
Cobwebs and skeletons in the closet, Baby,
they didn't just happen.
These are closed-door civil wars,
it doesn't take a genius
you hear the rain before you see it
(and everything you say sounds like bullshit).

Stop saying that I am stirring the pot.
We don't have to run out the clock.
I know you feel it in your gut,
we don't have to wait until we are enemies
to fall out of love.

On opposite ends of the couch
in the house
scrolling through a half-dead phone.
I wasn't planning my escape,
but it was time to go.
If love was all we needed,
I wouldn't be leaving.
We're both good people,
and there's no good reason
that you're under my skin
(and everything you say sounds like bullshit).

Stop saying I didn't give it all I got.
We don't have to run out the clock.
I know you feel it in your gut,
we don't have to wait until we are enemies
to fall out of love.

Currently listening to:
"Favourite Ex" by Maisie Peters

Track Forty-Nine

It took over a year, but the star the rock etched into my windshield finally burst and made itself known across the rest of the glass. It took over a year, but I'm cracking right behind it. So many chances to fix the damage before it got this bad, for both the window and myself, but I dragged my feet. That's what happens when you live inside a slow-drip apocalypse. The weight of the end of the world is on my shoulders. It's hard enough to exist on my couch, let alone exist on the Internet. So I pop in and out, like a lost signal—a dropped call. I stopped charging my phone overnight and I've been practicing goodbye speeches in front of the bathroom mirror. I wonder if I will ever be courageous enough to deliver them in front of someone other than my reflection. I don't know where I'm going, but I know I can't stand still much longer.

It took over a year, but the only person who hears about you now is my therapist. And you barely take up a minute of each session. When I first started coming, that wasn't the case and there was a branch just outside the office window that dangled by a thread. (Winter had been harsh to other living things besides me.) I always wondered if I would be there to witness when it finally snapped and crashed into the car parked below it. It took over a year, but one day the branch was gone. The tree looked even more bare and sick. Then time kept passing and spring arrived. That same tree I empathized with bloomed so brilliantly that endless petals covered the bark and filled in the gaps so much that you would never know it was grieving a limb all those months before. It was in front of that tree that I realized I no longer talked about you to my friends. Not everything that breaks needs to stay broken.

Currently listening to:
"Leave Me Again" by Kelsea Ballerini

Track Fifty

I was born in April
but I was due in May.
My mother says I arrived early
thanks to the steps
of the three-story walkup apartment
she had to trudge up and down every day.
I was born in April
inside the hospital
I still pass by in adulthood.
I was born in April
but I was due in May.
My father says the cherry blossoms
clung to their branches
longer than usual that year
because they wanted to meet me and
blanket me in their petals
like springtime snow.

Currently listening to:
"Mr. Carter" by Lil Wayne (featuring Jay-Z)

Track Fifty-One

I never broke anything that wasn't already on its way to ruin.

I almost said the quiet part out loud when we
were naked in your bed, but the setting was too
intimate, my armor and hair down,
your DNA under my nails.

I waited until we were dressed, but by then the
oven had preheated, and I figured I had already
eaten through too many uncomfortable meals in
my life to wreck this one too.

After cleaning up, I clutched the kitchen island
like a wooden door in the middle of a frigid sea.

All this time later,
I'm still picking your eyelashes
from between my teeth.
You're still finding my hair in your vacuum.

I never broke anything that wasn't already on its way to ruin.

Currently listening to:
"Pepper" by Death Cab for Cutie

Track Fifty-Two

My fight or flight responses have always been the same: *just stay busy.* Busy was my safety net. My go-to answer to all the questions I wanted to dodge. (*How are you? I'm busy!*) I've always been a master of outrunning the things I didn't want to face. I am the Queen of Postponement. My manic pace was often misinterpreted and praised as exceptional drive, but it was nothing but a false remedy—a coping mechanism that kept the memories and muck from resurfacing.

Then. The world stopped spinning for a collection of time. No one was around to kill the dandelions. Suddenly, they were sprouting everywhere. Suddenly, we were admiring their colors. Suddenly, they weren't weeds, they were flowers.

Turns out that I'm okay with being with myself even when I'm not busy, and now the only thing that haunts me is wondering how long this has been the case.

How long have I been running from nothing? How long ago could I have slowed down?

Currently listening to:
"rest in peace" by BLÜ EYES

Track Fifty-Three

I've kept the orchid alive for four months now /
I've been going to bed before 11 / I've been
falling asleep before midnight / I caught the
typo before it was too late / I forgave myself for
who I was in 2013 / I kept my mouth shut when
my voice wasn't needed / I screamed at the top
of my lungs when it was warranted / I didn't
text the narcissist back / I called my friends on
their birthdays / I didn't slip in the shower / No
broken bones when I tumbled down the attic
stairs / I began saying "no," instead of "maybe"
or "I'll see" when I knew it was never going to
be a "yes."

Currently listening to:
"Sparrow" by Emeli Sandé

Track Fifty-Four

The sapling you planted in your backyard as a child for a school project became a tree. You were alive to see it grow beyond your wildest imagination, ultimately eclipsing the height of your house.

It's still alive today, even though you're not.

It gets to feel the breeze, change with the seasons, stand upright, stretch its limbs, breathe, create a shadow. My grief has developed resentment toward this tree even though— statistically speaking—the tree was always going to outlive you.

Currently listening to:
"Hear You Me" by Jimmy Eat World

Track Fifty-Five

My biological clock wakes me
before my alarm.
Another night spent with the children
I never had;
they float faceless in the moats
of their sandcastles.
By the time my mother was my age,
she had three school-aged kids to raise.
And here I sit, contemplating
throwing away a plant I was gifted
because I don't want to be responsible
for keeping something else alive.
This life leaves me thirsty.
For it is not lush,
but incomplete, insatiable.
I look around and
I'm left parched by
the halfness of all
I've been coaxed into believing
will make me whole.

Currently listening to:
"Stoned at the Nail Salon" by Lorde

Track Fifty-Six

Addiction descended upon our home—
entered right through the front door.
An act of asymmetric warfare—
on the longest day of the year.
Took you as prisoner.
I never saw you again.

But I know,
I know that you gave it your all
even on the days you lost.
And I know,
I know you prayed to live
even on the days you begged to die.
And I know,
I know that you didn't mean
half the unfortunate things you screamed.

I know you were scared. So were we.

A wartorn family never returns
to who they used to be.
Battle-scarred, visiting the graveyard,
collecting sympathy cards.

Whoever claims addiction
would never target their street,
never met your courageous spirit,
never felt your brave heart beat.
Whoever claims you had this coming
never had to sing *happy birthday*
to an empty chair as the candle burns.

You fought like hell.
I promise, in all my retellings,
you die a hero's death.

Currently listening to:
"Keep Me in Your Heart" by Warren Zevon

Track Fifty-Seven

I've resigned to this sad day.
I have nowhere to be, so, let me be sad.
Let me cry over the slightest trouble
then explain to you that the tears have nothing
to even do with that inconvenience.
        (But you know that.)
Let me do my breathing exercises.
Let me apologize, assure you that this has
nothing to do with you.
        (But you know that.)
Let me wallow.
Let me mumble to myself.
Let my sleepy eyelids rest in this quiet gloom;
my insides are so loud and bright.
Let me be temporarily held down by this
invisible weight.
I'll successfully navigate through this smog, my
lighthouse.
You know that no matter how many times I
visit, I'll never make a home in worst-case
scenario.
I'll be back soon.
        (But you know that.)

Currently listening to:
"Trouble" by Cage the Elephant

Track Fifty-Eight

When I was growing up, the biggest lie I ever believed was that I would be able to outline every moment of my life, and that the trajectory of my life was going to be this fast-moving linear line upward, and that any pivots and dips off that course meant I was failing.

If you feel like you can never catch up lately . . . or that you'll never reach your goals . . . push through, little by little. Looking at the "big picture" could become overwhelming at times, making approaching that first step seem dauntingly impossible. Cross dates off calendars, check things off your to-do lists, take breaks, mess up, ask for help, and even start over. That is what I've started to do in my life. And wish I had been this gentle with myself sooner.

Every single person is living a life they never saw coming and has had to make sacrifices and postpone things and has had to grieve something or someone over the course of their life. What matters is our resiliency bubbled to the surface and we are here today, a monumental achievement in and of itself.

You don't have to be at your best to achieve greatness, but you do have to keep going. Even on days when I don't want to get out of bed, on days I feel like there is no point, I still get out of that bed. I still do the pointless things.

Because trying is progress. The dictionary has failed us because failure is not a backward direction. Asking for help is not a sign of weakness. And small, everyday wins are still victories worthy of celebration.

The great secret of continuing on even when you don't want to, or don't think you can, is that the version of yourself that will exist on the other side of this will always be grateful that you never gave up on yourself. You'll always be grateful that you kept going. You'll never regret it.

Currently listening to:
"Get Better" by Frank Turner

Track Fifty-Nine

Burnout is resting in our joints.
An emotional breakdown is lodged haphazardly
between our organs.
We've been off kilter all day.

But we're calm.

Now, being calm doesn't mean we are not
worried. We realize it might mean we're used to
worrying though. Used to anxious nights. Used
to being marooned on an island with only our
hurt feelings and problematic coping
mechanisms.

Being calm doesn't mean we're naïve to the
crisis at hand, but that we are well versed with
crises.

We're very worried, in fact, we're always
worried about one thing or another;
but we are unbothered.
Because we know even in the middle of the most
relentless of moments,
a better day can materialize any second.

Currently listening to:
"I Won't Back Down" by Tom Petty

Track Sixty

The more people think they know me, the more
I retreat back toward my familiar. To my people.
The people who don't expect anything from me—
who anchor me to who I was before I mattered
to strangers. They let me laugh or sob or nap.
They eat grilled cheese with me and see me in
my glasses. They allow me to be silly and
unkempt. They get annoyed with my messiness
and my tendency to leave wet towels on the
floor and call me out on my shit. I am
immediately myself again, calm and grounded.
The reverence I have for this special space
prevents me from ever buying into my own
hype. In fact, I bask in the dullness of who I
really am. The truth of the matter is, the ones
who think they know me, don't know me at all.
And the ones who know they know me will
always be there, even when I run out of clever
ways to say things.

Currently listening to:
"simple times" by Kacey Musgraves

Track Sixty-One

A child dies and a grieving mother is born.
She asks me why there isn't a better,
more fitting word for "unfair."

I tell her that I've found that
the more unnatural the experience,
the more asinine the word is
that's used to describe it.

I don't know why language
is designed this way;
to make the heartbreaking moments
we are so desperate
to find the right words for
all the more difficult.

I tell her that "grief" is the synonym for every
single word that is felt on the tips of our
tongues.

Currently listening to:
"Livin' for the Ones" by Bonnie Raitt

Track Sixty-Two

I wanted to fall asleep before the birds started
chirping but I drank an espresso / the next
episode started streaming / I know that actor
from somewhere / Wikipedia / I couldn't
remember if I blew out the candle or locked up
my car / I know my parents are not always
going to be here but I still can't call them back /
I need new pillows / I asked my phone if my
biological clock was still keeping time / what
does "geriatric" mean? / I have no idea where
my diamond ring is / the person sleeping next
to me might die before me one day / I count
everything I might, could, or already have lost
instead of sheep / speaking of / I misplaced my
birth certificate at a time when my family is
demanding more proof of life from me.

Currently listening to:
"24/7" by Kehlani

Track Sixty-Three

First, I fell in love with you. Then you took off
your sheep's clothing. Then you told me it was
all my fault. Then you didn't reach out on my
birthday. Then I changed my number. Then you
found me. Then I moved with no forwarding
address. Then the license plate ahead of me in
traffic shared your initials. Then I believed in
second chances. Then the coffee shop where we
were supposed to reunite unceremoniously
closed without warning. Not for the day, but for
good. Then you told me that I waste too much
energy twisting coincidences into signs. Then
we were done too. Not for just the day, but for
good.

Currently listening to:
"Oscar Winning Tears." by Raye

Track Sixty-Four

We are always teetering against the brink of Armageddon. We could be burning our tongue on soup, complaining that we are bored.

Then BOOM. *Insert life-altering event here.*

I reclaimed cemeteries and warzones. I sprinkled nectar and planted seeds and new smiles on top of what died. Now there are marigold gardens as far as our eyes can see. I promised you I'd come back, and I did. But I never promised I'd grow back the same.

How could I? I remember what happened here, beneath the new colors. The pandemonium. The grass stains and agony. I will never forget that just underneath this lush reset lies the disjointed bones of what once was.

You tell me I changed. Of course I did. The entire world shifted.

Currently listening to:
"Something to Sing About" by Sarah Michelle Gellar,
Amber Benson, and James Marsters (from Buffy the Vampire Slayer, *Season 6, Episode 7)*

Track Sixty-Five

I've been told that life only exists
where there is water.

And so,
when the first rain of spring
covers the cemetery ground,
and what was once frozen
forms mud puddles,
and the grass and soil get so drenched
that my feet sink toward you,
I am happy.

You are alive again.

Currently listening to:
"Together Again" by Janet Jackson

Track Sixty-Six

An excerpt from Cook's short story "Why I Left" from New Jersey Fan Club: Artists and Writers Celebrate the Garden State, *edited by Kerri Sullivan*

I began to avoid the Atlantic Ocean like some do mirrors. Sometimes when I was near the ocean, I cringed the same way I do when I find an old journal. I didn't want to face who I was or what I had been through. The ocean knew that person and all her secrets. The ocean would never let me forget that person, and reminders constantly washed up to my feet with the sea glass and pebbles.

If you're lucky to live long enough, you learn that you can spend too much time in one place. What used to recharge you begins to drain you. What used to bring you peace begins to haunt. Your safe haven becomes a crime scene. I couldn't stand behind the yellow tape anymore with this forced smile on my face, so I left.

I didn't run away, but I also didn't look in my rearview either. I didn't wield a match or leave a trail of gasoline behind me. I left gracefully and with a "see you soon." I left as I did so I would never have to leave for good. I wanted to come back. I wanted to love the ocean again. In order to repair my relationship with this town and myself, I had to leave.

Coming back is not the same as never leaving. If I had stayed, my resentment might have become irreversible. Distance helps us regain perspective. Now, I return here with appreciation and gratefulness in my heart. Comfort and familiarity have returned. I meet up with the ocean like I do an old friend who knows everything about me but still loves me anyway.

I am no longer jaded; I can see why so many visit. Because this place does hold magic, but you can only conjure it if you believe in it enough.

I believe again.

Currently listening to:
"Weird Goodbyes" by The National (featuring Bon Iver)

Track Sixty-Seven

I've been to so many funerals, I cannot walk by a
florist without smelling death.

It's a permanent sleep, but we call them wakes.
It's the worst hours for the living, but the first
three letters of the word spell out *fun*.

The younger the person, the more crowded the
parking lot; the more smokers outside the
entrance.

Why aren't there any windows in these rooms?
Why can't Death feel the sun on its face?
I've never seen a hearse broken down on the
side of the road, have you?

What do they do with the precious cargo inside
if the car dies too and can't finish the journey?

It's amazing that, even in death, we could still be
inconvenienced by something so unbelievably
mortal and run late to our own graves.

I always regret that I don't look at the body long
enough. If I look long enough, maybe I won't
forget that they had pierced ears and loved
Pepsi.

I regret using the term *body*. The throat that held
my favorite laugh deserves a sweeter name and
more years.

In lieu of flowers, give me my innocence back so I can walk past a florist and smell romance and spring; not loss and oblivion. In lieu of flowers, build me a time machine or get the fuck out.

Currently listening to:
"Into Each Life Some Rain Must Fall" by The Ink Spots
(featuring Ella Fitzgerald and Bill Kenny)

Track Sixty-Eight

A runaway out of runway.
Afraid to start over,
because what if peace doesn't
show up there either?

Stumbling backward instead of springing ahead.
The mind—a house of tripwires.
        Triggered when it's this warm in
        March.
        Triggered when I can smell dew in
        the morning.
My nose begins to bleed but I don't grab a
tissue—it'll stop on its own eventually.

        Everything stops on its own eventually.

I sit, wilting, while everything blossoms around
me. The more I'm told that I am not alone, the
further away everyone feels.

My best-laid plans always end up wrinkled.
My good intentions never translate well from
the paper.

I am a lot like the intersection in my hometown
that has had its traffic pattern changed four
times but still creates enough confusion to cause
accidents.

The show must go on—there is no offstage
standby.

Retreating inward but still showing up for you.
Still answering the phone though it feels like a
brick.

Still telling you what I need to hear.

Maybe we'll say it back and forth enough to
convince us both.

We're going to be just fine. Just fine.

Currently listening to:
"Help!" by The Beatles

Track Sixty-Nine

Blueberry tea makes me think of you. We never drank tea together, but once we shared so much blueberry champagne, the anthocyanin stained our teeth. The effervescent elixir possessed us to slow dance between the antique tables.

Even people who were never going to make it deserve a great memory or two, and this is ours.

The aroma leaving my warm cup tonight reminds me of that winery, and my skirt— adorned with yellow daisies. The scent, a composition of the start of spring and the end of fall, all at once—like the other two seasons don't exist in between.

That's something I've always secretly wished was true; that there was only spring and fall, and me and you.

Currently listening to:
"History of a Feeling" by Madi Diaz

Track Seventy

When your emergency contact dies and you
can't think of anyone else to list in their place.
When mail still comes in their name. When you
have to break the news to someone else, and
have to console them even though you're
inconsolable. When you hear their belly laugh,
smell their scent, swear you see them in a
crowd, and your brain forgets for less than a
second and you lose them all over again. When
they come to you in a dream. When they leave
you in a nightmare. When you have to switch
bills to your name and remember what day the
recycling gets picked up. When you are the only
one left who remembers that it is their birthday.
When psychiatrists want to pathologize grief
and say you have a disorder if you don't
"get better" within one year of their death.

Currently listening to:
"Wilder (We're Chained)" by Brandi Carlile

Track Seventy-One

The time has come for the colors to blend.
Laughter echoes from the throat of a friend
who is having a better day than I am.
I've always been quick to wax nostalgic.
Tonight's no different.

The sun is dropping
under the Newburgh-Beacon Bridge,
and I'm thinking about
all the lives I almost lived.
If we had made it, would I have had a kid?
The only time you ever truly loved me
was when the sky looked like this.

You used to have me
in your phone as "The One"
but you were always going or gone.
I was the home, you were the wrecker
who let the mice eat away the future
I kept folded in our dresser.

I always wanted to sleep with you without
setting an alarm. Wanted you to take your coat
off, lie around in our socks.

Wanted you to see my worth beneath my
damage. Was it suffocating, holding my hand
for as long as you managed?

I felt the storm coming, you know;
felt the atmospheric pressure plummet;
felt the final shifts of our season in my stomach.

We showered together that last morning;
by the afternoon you left.
I cleaned the sheets, made the bed.
There's a story I'm writing
based on actual events
but I don't want to give up the ending yet.

The only time you ever truly loved me
was when the sky looked like this; violet.

The leaving was quiet.
It was all so violent.

Did I always love watching the sunset,
or did I just like sitting still with you?

Currently listening to:
"Next to You" by John Vincent III

Track Seventy-Two

Moths flutter and fall.
Over and over again
they turn to dust on the porch.
We have more in common
with this invasive species than we realize.
Like a moth to a flame,
we have known a fatal attraction or two.
We have a tendency to run toward beautiful
lights that seem safe from a distance;
by the time we are close enough
to feel the heat, the danger,
we rarely consider retreating because pleasure
and pain hold hands in our brains.
And, like us, moths don't want to die,
they are just wired to escape darkness by any
means possible.

Currently listening to:
"817 Oakland Avenue" by Charlie Parr

Track Seventy-Three

When the words don't come even though the thoughts don't stop. When someone asks how you're doing, and you say "better" because "better" definitely doesn't mean "good" but it raises fewer alarms than "shitty." When you want to make your mark on the world but you can't collect yourself enough to refill your prescriptions or call your people back or sleep through the entire night.

You remember being twelve, in a contest with your friends to see who can stay underwater the longest before coming up for air.

You always won.

You realize you're still the friend who can remain submerged in the depths the longest. But you don't feel victorious anymore. You feel exhausted.

Currently listening to:
"My Mind & Me" by Selena Gomez

Track Seventy-Four

In some other timeline,
I find you in time,
turn you on your side.

In some other timeline,
I beat the sirens home
and you don't die alone.

In some other timeline,
you recover—
and no one needs to call your mother.

Currently listening to:
"Hurt" by Christina Aguilera

Track Seventy-Five

Surviving the unthinkable creates unthinkable aftereffects we must also live through. My aftermath was a rickety home held up by rubble and rage and rest and reincarnation. After months of bathing in tar and breathing in trauma, I took a deep breath and realized the air had recirculated enough to taste fresh again. This unmistakable shift seemingly happened overnight. But really, it was over a lifetime. I could taste a better tomorrow at the back of my throat. My regret was still beside me, but had lost steam, lowered its hands, and freed me from its decade-long chokehold. It was during this temporary time that I learned to fight because our ghosts don't need to breathe, or cry, or sweat to exist, but we do.

We will be stripped of our normalcy, over and over again, but our spirit will remain. In those moments, we are reminded that adaptability is our greatest strength. We are chameleons, clairvoyants, and shapeshifters, and we will always transform into who we need to be to make it through.

Currently listening to:
"The Next Right Thing" by Kristen Bell, from Disney's Frozen II

Track Seventy-Six

When the moon talks back, you listen:

"The day is over; let it go." / "A photo will never capture everything you encompass." / "It's okay to be blue sometimes." / "Even on days when you feel like you are floating away, there is gravity." / "There is power in mystery; you don't have to reveal every piece of yourself." / "Don't be a scapegoat; you are not the reason for another's bad behavior." / "Not every side of you will be appreciated or loved the same." / "You're a muse; appearing in poetry and dreams." / "You are always whole, regardless of what they say." / "Don't let people walk all over you."

Currently listening to:
"Trauma" by H.E.R. (featuring Cordae)

Track Seventy-Seven

Today marked a week of sleeping apart.
You met me at the park,
for a lark, for your amusement.
Said that you didn't know
what you were doin'.
But you always knew
what you were doin'.

A sinister loop,
mining social media for the scoop.
I was terrified of roller coasters
and you trapped me on one for a decade.
Survived all your end-of-day plagues—
swatted away the locusts and the frogs—
but you never called me brave.

And now I'm home
enjoying a movie
that I know you would hate;
it's in black and white
and they're smoking on the plane.

I wallowed,
swallowed pills laced with truth—
folded sharp glitter into my sad blues—
did not pick at the scab
around the exit wound.

Who were you foolin'?
You always knew what you were doin'.
I always knew what you were doin'.

Currently listening to:
"Over" by Ashanti

Track Seventy-Eight

I passed your driveway the other day on the way out of town. The ivy has become so overgrown, I can no longer see the wire fence I sliced my palm on the day of the Seafood Festival.

I don't know why (maybe I do), but I held my breath as I drove by your place. The burgundy curtains were still there. As the sun performed its daily swan song, I thought about iced mocha lattes and evening high tide swims and the casual absurdity of your magician hands.

Time can't be bottled, but humans try and try and try to preserve what can't stay. The supercut of our life together played until I cleared the bridge.

It's fitting that I split my existence between the ocean and the city. It's fitting that even with all the hopping around and time traveling you've managed to do, you never moved out of this tourist-trap town of broken clocks.

Currently listening to:
"Into You" by Julia Michaels

Track Seventy-Nine

I dream I am immortal and wake up wanting to
die. This body absorbs gray skies like it used to
do Ambien. Quickly. Sex under blankets always
feels more special. Maybe because that's how
the movies depict it. You never take pictures of
me. I wonder if that means anything. Everything
means something, so I suspect it does. By now
I've delivered more eulogies than wedding
toasts. Both are opposite ends of the same love
poem though. Two-feet-off-the-ground kisses
are cinematic. Two-knees-on-the-ground
prayers are desperate. Either experience leaves
us exposed, vulnerable. All of it molds us like
clay, squashes us like bugs, brings us back in a
way only miracles can.

Currently listening to:
"No One Changes" by Conor Oberst

Track Eighty

It's October all over again
and somewhere in this town
a young heart is being let down
for the first time in a parking lot.

I'm not sure a picture of us exists anymore,
and the older I get
the more that becomes my biggest regret.

Through all the prose and rabbit holes
I used to pray we'd catch red lights when you'd
take me home.
Now I dodge pigeons on my run
and I haven't drank in almost sixty months
but I remember when we warmed
wine on the stove
and the candle glow.

Our old radio station is just static now.
It's just so tragic how
I no longer know how
you spend your days
but I still think of you when
a Jack White song plays.

I didn't know who I was back then.
Back when I used to lean on NyQuil
because I couldn't lean on you.
Back when I spent my birthday wishes
wishing you'd grow up too.
Back when I pretended to not know about
the other women.
Back when Peter Pan told me he'd never
grow up, but I didn't listen.

Back when I knew you were leaving for the last
time, I paid close attention to your exit—
like I do the final colors of autumn
when I don't want it to go, but must let it.

Currently listening to:
"The Same Boy You've Always Known" by The White Stripes

Track Eighty-One

Remorse. The complicated compound of the good and the bad, an intricate mix of the best and the worst times.

I know what days I'll regret.

I'll regret the days I didn't kiss you or hug you or fuck you. I'll regret the days I sat across from you at dinner with nothing new to say or next to you on the couch with my eyes on a screen. I'll regret the days I forgot to mail something for you, or the days I snapped just because of the way you were chewing or the sound the nail clipper was making. I'll regret it to the point of forgetting the "why." I'll forget the reason for my behavior. I'll forget how broken I was, how lonely I was even with your companionship. I'll make myself the villain even though you never once villainized me.

I'll apologize for the cold gusts that hit your heart without warning throughout our time together, and you'll hold me and tell me you know I never meant to summon those winds.

Currently listening to:
"You Still Believe in Me" by The Beach Boys

Track Eighty-Two

I see the age on my face
more than the year before
but that's what time does, I know.

Parroted some vows in front of a crucifix
after walking down the aisle
when I was twenty-six
because I was told
that's the way a bride goes.

I think about the honeymoon
when the water soaked our phones.
You smiled and said,
"That's how the tide flows."

I always felt like a wobbly domino.
Like a kid in her mother's shoes
and dress-up clothes.

You wed yourself to me
before the meadows of my mind
became overgrown with weeds.

You loved me when I couldn't get out of bed
and I didn't know why;
before the nimbostratus clouds infected my sky.

When my mask decomposed
and revealed who I really was,
you held me and said,
"I'd do this all again—just because."

And I learned that peace
doesn't always announce itself,
it's hardly ever loud.
But one day you may find it
keeping you company on the couch.

Currently listening to:
"Hope It's You" by India Parkman

Track Eighty-Three

I will stand firm in your corner when no one else
is left but I will not be the one who loves you to
death.

I will practice forgiveness and in your life I will
invest but I will not be the one who loves you to
death.

I will scream hope to the sky until I am sore in
the chest but I will not be the one who loves you
to death.

I will pray for your recovery until my knees
need to rest but I will not be the one who loves
you to death.

I will offer my hand to pull you up from the
depths but I will not be the one who loves you
to death.

I will fight back against the statistics until I run
out of strength but I will not be the one who
loves you to death.

I will not surrender to the odds whenever I fail
to defend but I will not be the one who loves
you to death.

I will remind you to live until your very last
breath but I will not be blamed for how this
might end.

Currently listening to:
"Forest" by Caitlin Mahoney

Track Eighty-Four

Featured in The New York Times

Before I left forever,
I cleaned the dishes in the sink.

I knew I was leaving that morning.
I knew that I would never see that farm sink
again. I stood there and washed each item. Even
your roommate's skillet.
The water never got hot enough and the faucet
spattered in all directions.
I used to always complain about it.
A part of me wanted you to be haunted.
To come home and see me splattered
everywhere. Wanted to leave my wet
toothbrush next to yours.
A bigger part of me didn't want you to come
home to the mess we left behind.
So I stayed until the sink was empty.

To this day,
it remains the oddest thing
my broken heart has
ever made me do.

Currently listening to:
"Blue Skies" by Albert Hammond Jr.

Track Eighty-Five

On days everything feels heavy,
go outside, follow a floating leaf,
see where it is heading.

Watch as it scratches and tumbles
along the pavement—equipped with purpose,
yet still free and patient.

Mimic its motions,
stop and smell the roses
(as long as you're not allergic).
You have air under your steps,
you're guided by the wind.
You're warm thanks to
the sun flecks on your skin.

On these narrow blue streets,
where you were once sad,
you are now at peace—momentarily at least.
All because you followed
a crumpled, fallen leaf.

Currently listening to:
"Today We're the Greatest" by Middle Kids

Track Eighty-Six

I was your biggest fan but for me you'd only
say, "I'll get there if I can."

You're still out constructing your land
of make believe. Still auditioning understudies
with the same astrological sign as me.
The only thing that has ever
been consistent about you is your type.
Pretty, manic-depressive,
filled with malleable strife.
You seek out raconteurs who can preserve you
in ambered nostalgia.
You fall for the hands that pay homage,
that penstroke your ego.
You strike our nerves and we strike gold.
You take credit for talent you'll never hold.
Hate to break it to you, Columbus,
but you didn't discover shit;
you just stumbled upon preexisting greatness
and claimed ownership.

But lucky, lucky you.
Now you have the poets and the singers telling stories
about you.

Currently listening to:
"Telling Stories" by Tracy Chapman

Track Eighty-Seven

Distance from the ground can drown out the most unpleasant side effects of reality. That's why I like being in places like Manhattan or Boston or Nashville; I prefer waking up hundreds of feet above the chaos humanity creates on the street. From up here, we seem half decent. Determined, like we have direction, and know exactly where we are going. From up here, I can't hear the confusion, the rage, the hate. From up here I can't feel the despair and division. From up here, we seem to be on even ground, to have our shit collectively together. The moment the elevator dings and my feet hit the crooked pavement the sensory overload is enough to make my ears pop. I am overcome with how messy the mayhem is, how cluttered and uneven we've become, how we rush past one another without eye contact, even though we are all just trying to get to where we are going without incident, in one piece. I cross against the light and join the masses.

Currently listening to:
"Fake Happy" by Paramore

Track Eighty-Eight

I bought a bloodstone after it fell apart.
Instead of getting bangs or getting on a plane.
The stone wasn't as green as the
chrysanthemums sitting nearby on the counter
but the woman who sold it to me
said it would protect me against self-sabotage.

I sewed it into my bracelet to keep my pulse
company. I wore it in the rain, as sorrow washed
down my face. I stood with it in the wind, and
let the air redirect me. We both recharged in the
moonlight, in the sunshine, and in the mud.

To this day, I am not sure if I had just
succumbed to the placebo effect.
But one thing I know for certain is that the
bloodstone proved that I could believe in
something—trust something—with my whole
heart again.

And that gave me hope.

Currently listening to:
"My Way" by Aloe Blacc

Track Eighty-Nine

We're still children when our laces come undone and we lean down to tie our shoes. And we're still children when we visit our parents and they comment on our weight or our eating habits. And we're still children when we have to bury them. And we're still children when we count how many of the passing cars have trees tied to their roofs. And we're still children when that nostalgic steam rages out of our ears when we see our sisters wearing our sweaters. And we're still children when we speak into fans and when we hop over cracks in the sidewalk. And we're still children when we're sick, eating pastina in bed. And we're still children when snowflakes touch our tongues. And we're still children when we stand along the perimeter of a carousel and a tiny hand waves to us as they spin by, and we wave back.

Currently listening to:
"Better Days" by Chris Rockwell

Track Ninety

Put the needle back on the record.
It's supposed to sting.

Nonfatal wounds can hurt so badly
in the moment that you can be
convinced you're dying.
It's not fair.
But it is happening.
It's not good right now.
But it was good before.
It will be good again.
But in between today and then
a lot of shit can happen.
You will be rattled. You will be tested.
An intrusive voice will try to brainwash you
into thinking that it will never get better.
But it does.

Flip the record over.
There is still more music to hear.

Currently listening to:
"superhuman" by Bishop Briggs

Track Ninety-One

I am not brave.
I am patient with my panic.

Doing something productive with this sadness
doesn't make me less sad, but it does give my
sadness purpose. And purpose gives me
direction, and every step—whether it's forward
or not—motivates me to take another step. And
on days the motivation isn't there, and the air
starts to evaporate from the room again, a fail-
safe inside of me activates: discipline.

I'm not brave.
I'm purposeful.
I'm patient.
I'm disciplined
in the art of doing things scared.

Currently listening to:
"Lose Yourself" by Eminem

Track Ninety-Two

How dare you, Time,
for running out
when we weren't looking.

In the middle of a smile—
in the midst of a sigh.

How dare you, Time,
for continuing on forever
but not letting us do the same.

We were so happy here, all together—
the music was just getting good.

No matter our grief,
we must thank you, Time,
for gifting us what you were able.

We know—
there will never be enough
of you to go around.

Currently listening to:
"Carousel" by Miranda Lambert

You have reached
the end of Side A

SIDE B

The Remixes

Track One

midnight

start

s

a

war

in   M y

min

d   b ut   I'll

be okay

Currently listening to:
"Tired" by beabadoobee

Track Two

the dawn

blanket ... s

th ... is

dystopian

world i ... n

hope ... f

u ... l

fingerprints

Currently listening to:
"If I Ruled the World (Imagine That)" by Nas (featuring Lauryn Hill)

Track Three

best friends

go

missing
without a why

taken away from us

Like

our innocence

Currently listening to:
"Closing Time" by Semisonic

Track Four

a long

close look

un   tangles

The

barbed wire

Li e

Currently listening to:
"Resentment" by Madi Diaz

Track Five

I ▇▇▇▇▇▇▇▇▇▇▇▇
▇▇▇▇▇▇▇▇▇▇▇▇
▇▇▇▇▇▇
▇▇▇▇▇▇▇▇▇▇▇
▇▇▇▇▇▇▇▇▇▇ w ▇

▇▇▇▇▇▇▇▇▇▇▇▇▇ ill ▇▇▇
▇▇▇▇▇▇▇▇▇▇▇
▇▇▇▇▇▇▇▇▇▇▇▇▇▇
▇▇▇▇▇
▇▇▇▇▇▇▇▇▇
▇▇▇▇▇▇▇▇▇▇▇
▇▇▇▇▇▇▇ love ▇▇▇▇
▇▇▇▇▇▇▇▇▇▇▇
▇▇▇▇
▇▇▇▇▇▇▇▇▇▇▇▇
▇▇▇▇▇▇▇▇
▇▇▇▇▇▇▇

▇▇▇▇▇▇▇▇▇▇▇▇▇▇▇

▇▇▇▇▇▇▇▇▇
▇▇▇▇▇▇▇▇▇
▇▇▇▇▇▇▇▇▇▇▇
▇▇▇▇▇▇▇▇▇▇▇
▇▇▇

▇▇▇▇▇▇▇▇▇▇▇▇▇
▇▇▇▇▇▇▇▇▇▇▇▇
▇▇

You ███
in t███████ o████ the afterlife,
████████████████████████████
No matter how ████████████
lonely ████████
████████████████████████████

Currently listening to:
"Open Your Heart" by Madonna

Track Six

m
y
heart
is a
force
G   on
e
cold.

Tell me

The

sparkle

I s

not dead

Currently listening to:
"hope is a dangerous thing for a woman like me to have—but I have it"
by Lana Del Rey

Track Seven

I

burn

the   book about

u   s   an

d   write

of

life   beyond

that   static

and

I'm alive.

Currently listening to:
"Happier Than Ever" by Billie Eilish

Track Eight

you

whisper

to

m y

sad

heart

Currently listening to:
"Better Place" by Rachel Platten

Track Nine

It's ███ hard ███
███

█████
█████
███ t ██ o ██
██ smile ███
██ and ████
█████
█████
██ feel ███
█████
█████
██ Our ████
█████ best
██ i ████
n ████
███ a ██ human ██
█████
██ world ███

█████

Currently listening to:
"Past Life" by Maggie Rogers

Track Ten

brittle heart s

still

dream

Currently listening to:
"So Many Tears" by 2Pac

Track Eleven

blue
skies
catch fire
and people

are not
the same. silver linings

And
fluffy clouds

m a y

go dark.
w e

search

for

s o me

thing to celebrate

Currently listening to:
"Ain't No Mountain High Enough" by Marvin Gaye and
Tammi Terrell

Track Twelve

snow

tasted warm

to

a broken

Jack Frost

Currently listening to:
"Christmas Makes Me Cry" by Kacey Musgraves

Track Thirteen

█████████████████████████████
████

█████████████████████████████
██████████ time ██████████████
█████████████████████████████
███████████████████████████████
████████████████████████████
████████████████████████████
█████████████████████████
████ slowly ███████████████████
██████████████████████████
████ dangle ████████████████ s,
preferr████ing ██████████ t███ o█
████████████████████

█ delay ██ the inevitable ████████

Currently listening to:
"100 Years" by Five for Fighting

Track Fourteen

We ███████████████████████████
████████████████

███████████████████████████████
███████████████████████████████
████████████████████████ pump ████████
█████████████ love ██ through
█████████████ years ████████████
█████████████████████████ and █
short days ████████████ and ██████████
continue to carry|

█ love ███ through ██████████████████
███████████████████████████████
█ broken ██████ time|

Currently listening to:
"Unchained Melody" by The Righteous Brothers

Track Fifteen

Cowritten with Christopher Andrews

Summer

Currently listening to:
"Iris" by Goo Goo Dolls

Track Sixteen

the

wayward one

s

ar   e

Doubtful.
the

y

never trust
why

Currently listening to:
"Different" by Ximena Sariñana

Track Seventeen

Currently listening to:
"If You Don't Like the Story Write Your Own" by Witt Lowry

Track Eighteen

I ███████████ miss ███████████████████
████████████████████████████████████
████ you ███████████████████████████
████████████████████████ so badly
████████████████████████████████
████████████████████████████████
████████████████████████████████
████████████████ my ████████████
████████████████████████████████
beautiful ████ angel ██████████████
████████████████ i ████ n ██ the
ground ██████████████████

████████████████████████████████
████████████████

Currently listening to:
"Fire and Rain" by James Taylor

Track Nineteen

████████████████████████
████████████████ ████
███████████ I ████████████
hid ████████████ your ███

███ laugh █

████ u ██ n ████████
███ d ████ er ██████
███████████████
████████████████
█ my ████

████████████ pillow█
███████ .
I ████ woke up
████████

████████████████
██████████████████
████████████████
████████████████ less█

████████████
██████████████████
████████████

█████████████████
███████████████████
████████████████
████████████
███████████ alone█

████████████████

Currently listening to:
"Chasing Cars" by Snow Patrol

Track Twenty

soft

time

sit still next to

me .

Don't

sway

ahead

Currently listening to:
"929" by Halsey

Track Twenty-One

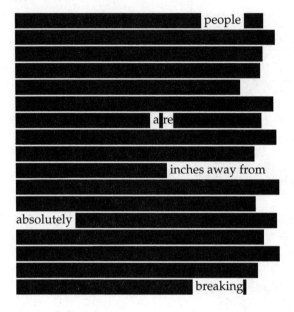

people

are

inches away from

absolutely

breaking

Currently listening to:
"Have You Ever Seen the Rain?" by Creedence Clearwater Revival

Track Twenty-Two

beautiful

words

Can

make   sense

of

death

Currently listening to:
"Yesterday" by The Beatles

Track Twenty-Three

You ██████████████████ c █ a ████████
████████████ n █████████████████████
████ n ██ o █████ t █ fault ███████████
████████████████████████ the ██████
████████████████████████ rain│

██████████████████████████████ for █
████████████████████████████████
████████████████████

████████ forgetting to water ████████
██████████████████████████
████████████████████████████
██████████████████████████████
████████████████████████████████
██████████████ the desert █████
████████████████████████████
██████████████████

Currently listening to:
"Voice In My Head" by Alessia Cara

144

Track Twenty-Four

an odd

empty

smile

grips   a person

w h o

is wondering if

th e flowers

worry about death

to o

Currently listening to:
"Spirits" by The Strumbellas

Track Twenty-Five

I █████████████████████████████
████████████████████████████
████████████████████████████
██

████ step into ████████████ lace ████████
███████████████████ and ████████
████ love ████████████████████
███████████████████

███████████████ and ████████████
██████████████████████████
██████████████

█ Return home ████████████████
███████████████ to ████████████
your heart ██████████████████████
████████████████████████
████████████████████████

Currently listening to:
"1950" by King Princess

Track Twenty-Six

my
temperature

change s

from

fire

t o

ice

Currently listening to:
"Fuck You" by Lily Allen

Track Twenty-Seven

your

heart

is magic

to me

Currently listening to:
"The First Time Ever I Saw Your Face" by Roberta Flack

Track Twenty-Eight

Sometimes ███████████████
██████ you'll feel ███ a ████████

████████████████████████
███████████████████████ draft
████████████████████

█████████████████████████████
██ o ████████ f █████████████████
████████████████████████

███████████████████ luck████ while
███████████████ sitting in a cold ████ room ████
█████████████████████████████
████

Currently listening to:
"I Think I'm Growing?" by FLETCHER

Track Twenty-Nine

above my head

the

dead

sing

to remind

m   e

o f

memories

 between us

Currently listening to:
"One Sweet Day" by Mariah Carey and Boyz II Men

Track Thirty

Our shaky
bones

are ill-prepared
as we
dance t
o ward

death

Currently listening to:
"Paradise By the Dashboard Light" by Meat Loaf

Track Thirty-One

mourning We bury

live s

our

hearts

ne

ver touched

Currently listening to:
"Lift Me Up" by Rihanna

Track Thirty-Two

no
one e

g e t s

to
the grave

un touched

o r

unscathed

Currently listening to:
"Slippin'" by DMX

Track Thirty-Three

the

fair-weather

dead

mispronounce

loneliness
th   e
y
ca
l   l

it

home

they

can finally rest

Currently listening to:
"Why" by Rascal Flatts

Track Thirty-Four

shower

Apologi e

s

on t o

the world

and

be

a

guiding

light

Currently listening to:
"I Am Light" by India.Arie

Track Thirty-Five

█████ a █████████████

███████████████████████
███████████████████████
███████████████████████

startled ███ bird █████████
█████████████████████████
█████████████████████████
█████████████████████

██████████ watched m ████ e ████
█████████████████████████
█████████████████████
███████████████████████

████████ f █ l ████ y.

I kept g █ o █ ing █████████████

████████████ I survived █████████

Currently listening to:
"Come Fly With Me" by Frank Sinatra

Track Thirty-Six

self-

love

accumulates inside of me,

I clumsily

recover

The

gold

in

m   y

rainbow

Currently listening to:
"Dog Days Are Over" by Florence + The Machine

Track Thirty-Seven

You ▮▮▮▮▮ a▮▮ re ▮▮▮▮ the
blizzard ▮▮▮▮ behind ▮▮▮▮▮▮▮▮
▮▮▮▮▮▮▮▮▮▮▮▮▮▮▮▮▮▮▮▮
▮▮▮▮▮▮▮▮▮▮▮▮▮▮▮▮▮▮
▮▮▮▮▮▮▮▮ m▮▮ y ▮▮▮▮▮
▮▮▮▮▮▮▮▮▮▮▮▮▮▮▮▮▮▮
▮▮▮▮▮▮▮▮▮▮▮▮▮▮▮▮▮▮▮▮
▮▮▮▮▮▮▮▮▮▮▮

▮▮▮▮▮▮▮▮▮▮▮▮▮▮▮▮▮
▮▮▮▮▮▮▮▮▮▮▮▮▮▮▮▮▮▮
▮▮▮▮▮▮▮ frostbit▮▮▮▮▮
▮▮▮ t ▮▮▮▮▮ e ▮▮ n▮
▮▮▮▮▮▮▮▮▮▮▮▮▮▮▮▮
▮▮▮▮▮▮▮▮▮▮▮▮▮▮▮
▮▮▮▮▮▮▮▮▮▮▮▮▮▮▮▮
▮▮▮▮▮▮▮▮▮▮▮▮▮▮▮▮
▮▮▮▮▮▮▮▮▮▮▮▮▮▮▮▮

▮▮▮▮▮▮▮▮▮▮▮▮▮▮▮▮▮
▮▮▮▮▮▮▮▮▮▮▮▮▮▮▮▮
▮▮▮▮▮▮▮▮▮▮▮▮▮▮▮
▮▮▮ heart ▮▮▮▮▮▮▮▮▮
▮▮▮

Currently listening to:
"The Steps" by HAIM

Track Thirty-Eight

I

ta
k e the tired

step

s

b

ack
t o

my

s e
l

f

Currently listening to:
"Programs" by Mac Miller

Track Thirty-Nine

grief

pierces

like a knife

Currently listening to:
"It's So Hard to Say Goodbye to Yesterday" by Boyz II Men

Track Forty

You are ████████████
████████ the clock ███████

██████████████
██████████████
I ████████████
███████████████

█████████████████████

██████████████████████
███████████████████████
                    keep ████████
resetting ███████ . ████ I ██████
████████████████████████
████████████████ Long█
███████████████
████████

████ to ████████████
████ n ██ ever ████████
███████████████████

████ waste ██████████████
████████████ a ████████
████ minute ███████████

Currently listening to:
"You're Still The One" by Shania Twain

Track Forty-One

a

change

of

heart

c   an

be

a beautiful

fix

Currently listening to:
"One Step at a Time" by Jordin Sparks

Track Forty-Two

this

sharp

haphazard

world

we

have to li

ve   in   is

making me sick

Currently listening to:
"This Is America" by Childish Gambino

Track Forty-Three

My

smile

with

stood

impossible

pain

Currently listening to:
"Home" by Mike Posner

Track Forty-Four

Our
mundane moment s

filled with

beautiful

slow

blinks

Currently listening to:
"You're In My Heart" by Rod Stewart

Track Forty-Five

lessons

rise

u p fr

o m

under

bo t h

dreadful and good

days

Currently listening to:
"Long Walk Home" by Bruce Springsteen

Track Forty-Six

I lost

myself trying to f

i n

d

The

answer in

you

Currently listening to:
"Interlude" by Kelsea Ballerini

Track Forty-Seven

████ the ████████████████████████
dark████████████████████████████
████████████████████████████████
████████████████████████████████
████

████ doesn't worry ████████████

████████████████████████████████
████████████████████████████████
████████████████████████████████████
████████ the ██████████

████████████████ special ones ████████
████████████████████████████████
████████████████████████████████

Currently listening to:
"Anything Can Happen" by Tors

Track Forty-Eight

Cowritten with Carly Moffa

I ▮▮ keep ▮▮▮
▮▮▮▮▮▮▮
▮▮▮ skeletons ▮▮ close ▮ by,
▮▮▮▮▮
▮▮▮▮▮
▮▮▮▮
▮▮▮ like ▮▮▮

▮▮▮▮▮
▮▮▮▮▮
▮▮▮▮
▮▮▮▮▮▮
▮▮▮

▮▮▮▮
▮▮
▮▮ half-dead ▮▮
▮▮▮▮▮
▮▮▮▮
▮▮▮▮
▮▮▮▮
▮▮▮▮
▮▮▮▮
▮▮▮▮▮▮▮

▮▮▮▮▮
▮▮▮▮▮
▮▮▮▮
▮▮▮ enemies
▮▮▮

Currently listening to:
"everyone at this party" by Camila Cabello

Track Forty-Nine

windshield

glass

a   t

my feet.

The

world

stopped

f o   r

a minute   .   I

dangled by

the

crash   the car

was

filled

██████████████ w █ i █

th ██████████████████

████ my friends ████████████

███████████

Currently listening to:
"Last Kiss" by Pearl Jam

Track Fifty

April

was born
inside

a

cherry blossom

petal

Currently listening to:
"April In Paris" by Ella Fitzgerald and Louis Armstrong

Track Fifty-One

I am a quiet

wreck

in the sea

still

finding my

way

Currently listening to:
"Introvert" by Little Simz

Track Fifty-Two

w   e

Postpone

the   e   nd   o   f

The world

and

admir   e

the

flowers

a   s   long   as

w   e

c   a   n

Currently listening to:
"I Melt With You" by Modern English

Track Fifty-Three

I've been
falling
for
y ou
at the top
of my lungs

I tumble
saying
"yes."

Currently listening to:
"The Best" by Tina Turner

Track Fifty-Four

your

wild

imagination ultimately

create s grief

Currently listening to:
"Jack's Obsession" by Danny Elfman and the cast from
The Nightmare Before Christmas

Track Fifty-Five

wake me
before
they
plant
me alive
in
a hole

Currently listening to:
"I Wonder What Became of Me" by Diahann Carroll

Track Fifty-Six

w   e

gave it our all

And

were

never

target   s

o

f

an empty

██████████████████

█ promise, in all my retellings █

██████████████████

Currently listening to:
"skinny dipping" by Sabrina Carpenter

Track Fifty-Seven

Let me ▮▮▮▮▮▮▮

▮▮▮▮▮ apologize ▮▮▮▮

▮▮▮ to myself.
Let m▮e ▮▮▮ rest
▮ inside ▮▮▮

▮▮▮ this ▮▮
lighthouse▮
▮▮ o ▮ r ▮▮
▮ I'll never make ▮ i ▮ t ▮

▮ back ▮

Currently listening to:
"I Walk The Line" by Johnny Cash

Track Fifty-Eight

I   outline

my life

little by little

with

sacrifices

and

great

failure s

And

victories .

Currently listening to:
"this is me trying" by Taylor Swift

Track Fifty-Nine

Currently listening to:
"The Baddest" by Big Sean

Track Sixty

a familiar

stranger

to

myself ,
I

don't know me at all.

Currently listening to:
"Every Day Is Exactly the Same" by Nine Inch Nails

Track Sixty-One

grieving

isn't

a   n

unnatural   experience,

it

is designed

to   b e

felt

Currently listening to:
"So Far Away" by Carole King

Track Sixty-Two

I ▮▮▮d fall asleep ▮▮▮▮▮ next to ▮ ... y ▮ ou a n d misplace time

Currently listening to:
"Say You Love Me" by Jessie Ware

Track Sixty-Three

love

found me in

s i d e

a

second chance

Currently listening to:
"Hands Down" by Dashboard Confessional

Track Sixty-Four

war

stains

The

world

Currently listening to:
"War Pigs" by Black Sabbath

Track Sixty-Five

███████████ life ███████
███████████

██████
██████████████
██████████████
████████████

██████ puddles
███████████████████

█ at my feet ██████████ ,
I am ██████

██████ alive again

Currently listening to:
"How Far I'll Go" by Auli'i Cravalho, from Disney's **Moana**

Track Sixty-Six

Atlanti   s

cringed   when

secrets

washed up

to

haunt

th   e m

the ocean

town

never

returned

but still

h a

s magic

you can conjure if you believe in it enough

Currently listening to:
"Shore Towns" by Brian Erickson

Track Sixty-Seven

many

hours for the living

are

inconvenienced by

mortal

regret

Currently listening to:
"Count Your Blessings Instead of Sheep" by Bing Crosby
from the 1954 film White Christmas

Track Sixty-Eight

peace

Stumbl e s ahead

som

e

times but still

c

o

M███e███s██ back ███████ to
███ us ██

Currently listening to:
"breathin" by Ariana Grande

Track Sixty-Nine

we

slow dance between

the start and the end of

i t

all

Currently listening to:
"Slow Dancing in a Burning Room" by John Mayer

Track Seventy

your

name

break s me

i hear

i t

in m y

nightmare s

and remember

you r

death

Currently listening to:
"Tears in Heaven" by Eric Clapton

Track Seventy-One

time

Laugh s a nd

I am

nostalgic

f

o

r

the lives I almost lived.

the future

ke

ep

s

suffocating

m e

in my

morning

sheets,

I   want to

just   sit   still

Currently listening to:
"I Was Here" by Beyoncé

Track Seventy-Two

Over and over again

we realize

our brains
want to
escape darkness

Currently listening to:
"Cold Day In The Sun" by Foo Fighters

Track Seventy-Three

When you

make

i t

through the entire night

submerge in the depths

o f victor y

Currently listening to:
"Close My Eyes" by Mariah Carey

Track Seventy-Four

 find time to call your mother

Currently listening to:
"Don't Tell My Mom" by Reneé Rapp

Track Seventy-Five

unthinkable

shift s happen

. But

temporary

normalcy

remind s

me

we will

always

make it through

Currently listening to:
"Better Than We Found It" by Maren Morris

Track Seventy-Six

capture th e

days

reveal

yourself.

in

poetry

Currently listening to:
"Road to Joy" by Bright Eyes

Track Seventy-Seven

You

didn't know

I was terrified

for a decade.

you never

a

s

k

ed

m   e

Currently listening to:
"Love The Way You Lie Part III" by Skylar Grey

Track Seventy-Eight

I

no longer

breath   e

in

the

absurdity o   r

try and try

and try to

move

broken clocks

Currently listening to:
"Piece by Piece (Idol Version)" by Kelly Clarkson

Track Seventy-Nine

immortal

skies

deliver

cinematic

miracles

Currently listening to:
"Solitude" by Billie Holiday

Track Eighty

a young heart

becomes

old .
It's tragic how

birthday wishes

pretend to

listen

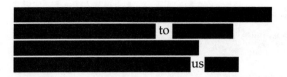

Currently listening to:
"Stay Together for the Kids" by Blink-182

Track Eighty-One

██████████ complicated ████████████
██████████████████████████████████████
████████████

██████████████ regret█

████████████████████████████████████
███████████████████ sat ██████████
████████████████████████████████████
████████████████████████████████████
████████████████████████████████████
██████ chewing ████████████████████
████████████████████████████████████
██████████████████████████████████
████████████████████████████████████
██████████████████████ on █████████
███████████████████ you ██ r
████████████████

██████████████ cold gust ██████████
heart █████████████████████████████
████████████████████████████████████
████████████████████████████████████.

Currently listening to:
"You Learn" by Alanis Morissette

Track Eighty-Two

the year

became overgrown with

love
and

revealed

peace

Currently listening to:
"Auld Lang Syne" by Ingrid Michaelson

Track Eighty-Three

I will ████████████████████
████████████████████
██

████████████████████
████████████████████
██

████████████████ love you
██

until my ████
████████████████████
██

████████████████
████████████████
██

██████████████████
██████████████████
██████

██████████████████
██████████████
███

█████████████ very last
breath █████████████
████

Currently listening to:
"Sun to Me" by Zach Bryan

Track Eighty-Four

Before

you

I used to

come home

to

A big

mess .

I was empty

Currently listening to:
"Cover Me Up" by Jason Isbell

Track Eighty-Five

everything

tumbles
along
patient

steps
guide
You to
your

peace

Currently listening to:
"I Didn't Know My Own Strength" by Whitney Houston

Track Eighty-Six

a

Pretty

pen

discover s

great

stories

Currently listening to:
"Non-Stop" by the original Broadway cast of
Hamilton: An American Musical

Track Eighty-Seven

o h
s a d

humanity

we

can't
see

how messy
and uneven we've become

Currently listening to:
"You'll Never Walk Alone" by Elvis

Track Eighty-Eight

I bought ███████████████████
████████████████████████████
██████ w █████████████████
h █ a █ t ████████████ y o ████ u ███
███████████ sold ███ me
████████████████████████████

████████████ y █████ o █████ u ███
████████████████████████████████
████████████████████████████
████████████████ charged ████
████████████████████████

████████████████████████
████ m █ e ██████████████
████████ in ████████████
blood ██████████████████
████████████████████████████
████████████

████████████████████

Currently listening to:
"If Your Girl Only Knew" by Aaliyah

Track Eighty-Nine

We'll undo

our parents

weight

And

rage when we

r a i s e

our children

Currently listening to:
"Before I Have a Daughter" by Bre Kennedy

Track Ninety

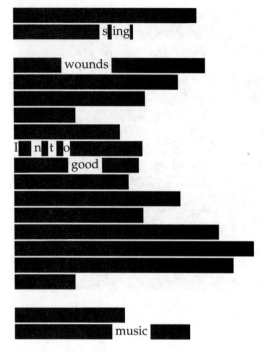

s ing

wounds

I n t o

good

music

Currently listening to:
"The Mixtape" by Jack's Mannequin

Track Ninety-One

brave

sadness

activates

brave

art

Currently listening to:
"Grace" by Pamela Flores

Track Ninety-Two

the ████████████ e█ n█ ██ d.

████ thank you ████

Currently listening to:
"Famous Last Words" by Billy Joel

Blackout Poetry Key

1. Midnight starts a war in my mind but I'll be okay
2. The dawn blankets this dystopian world in hopeful fingerprints
3. Best friends go missing without a why / taken away from us like our innocence
4. A long close look untangles the barbed wire lie
5. I will love you into the afterlife, no matter how lonely
6. My heart is a force gone cold. Tell me the sparkle is not dead
7. I burn the book about us and write of life beyond that static and I'm alive
8. You whisper to my sad heart
9. It's hard to smile and feel our best in a human world
10. Brittle hearts still dream
11. Blue skies catch fire and people are not the same. Silver linings and fluffy clouds may go dark. We search for something to celebrate
12. Snow tasted warm to a broken Jack Frost
13. Time slowly dangles / preferring to delay the inevitable
14. We pump love through years and short days and continue to carry love through broken time
15. We paint our love in spring and rehearse for summer
16. The wayward ones are doubtful. They never trust why
17. If a story pulls at you enough, you have to share it
18. I miss you so badly my beautiful angel in the ground
19. I hid your laugh under my pillow. I woke up less alone
20. Soft time / sit still next to me. Don't sway ahead
21. People are inches away from absolutely breaking
22. Beautiful words can make sense of death
23. You cannot fault the rain for forgetting to water the desert
24. An odd empty smile grips a person who is wondering if the flowers worry about death too

25. I step into lace and love and return home to your heart
26. My temperature changes from fire to ice
27. You heart is magic to me
28. Sometimes you'll feel a draft of luck while sitting in a cold room
29. Above my head the dead sing to remind me of memories between us
30. Our shaky bones are ill-prepared as we dance toward death
31. In mourning we bury lives our hearts never touched
32. No one gets to get grave untouched or unscathed
33. The fair-weather dead mispronounce loneliness / they call it home—they can finally rest
34. Shower apologies onto the world and be a guiding light
35. A startled bird watched me fly. I kept going / I survived
36. Self-love accumulates inside of me, I clumsily recover the gold in my rainbow
37. You are the blizzard behind my frostbitten heart
38. I take the tired steps back to myself
39. Grief pierces like a knife
40. You are the clock I keep resetting. I long to never waste a minute
41. A change of heart can be a beautiful fix
42. This sharp haphazard world we have to live in is making me sick
43. My smile withstood impossible pain
44. Our mundane moments filled with beautiful slow blinks
45. Lessons rise up from under both the dreadful and good days
46. I lost myself trying to find the answer in you
47. The dark doesn't worry the special ones
48. I keep skeletons close by, like half-dead enemies
49. Windshield glass at my feet. The world stopped for a minute. I dangled by the crash / the car was filled with my friends

50. April was born inside a cherry blossom petal

51. I am a quiet wreck in the sea. Still finding my way

52. We postpone the end of the world and admire the flowers as long as we can

53. I've been falling for you at the top of my lungs / I tumble saying "yes."

54. Your wild imagination ultimately creates grief

55. Wake me before they plan me alive in a hole

56. We gave it our all and were never targets of an empty promise, in all my retellings

57. Let me apologize to myself. Let me rest inside this lighthouse or I'll never make it back

58. I outline my life little by little with sacrifices and great failures and victories

59. Rest or break are our only two choices

60. A familiar stranger to myself, I don't know me at all

61. Grieving isn't an unnatural experience, it is designed to be felt

62. I fall asleep next to you and misplace time

63. Love found me inside a second chance

64. War stains the world

65. Life puddles at my feet, I am alive again

66. Atlantis cringed when secrets washed up to haunt them. The ocean town never returned but still has magic you can conjure if you believe in it enough

67. Many hours for the living are inconvenienced by mortal regret

68. Peace stumbles ahead sometimes but still comes back to us

69. We slow dance between the start and the end of it all

70. Your name breaks me / I hear it in my nightmare and remember your death

71. Time laughs and I am nostalgic for the lives I almost lived. The future keeps suffocating me in my morning sheets, I want to just sit still

72. Over and over again we realize our rains want to escape darkness

73. When you make it through the entire night / submerge in the depths of victory

74. Find time to call your mother

75. Unthinkable shifts happen. But temporary normalcy reminds me we will always make it through

76. Capture the days / reveal yourself in poetry

77. You didn't know I was terrified for a decade. You never asked me

78. I no longer breathe in the absurdity or try and try and try to move broken clocks

79. Immortal skies deliver cinematic miracles

80. A young heart becomes old. It's tragic how birthday wishes pretend to listen to us

81. Complicated regret sat chewing on your cold gust heart

82. The year became overgrown with love and revealed peace

83. I will love you until my very last breath

84. Before you I used to come home to a big mess. I was empty

85. Everything tumbles along—patient steps guide you to your peace

86. A pretty pen discovers great stories

87. Oh sad humanity / we can't see how messy and uneven we've become

88. I bought what you sold me / you charged me in blood

89. We'll undo our parents weight and rage when we raise our children

90. Sing wounds into good music

91. Brave sadness activates brave art

92. The End. Thank you

Acknowledgments

There's not much else to say because I've said it in the pages. Thank you to my parents, family, friends, and readers. The last eight years have been such a wonderful, life-fulfilling experience. Concluding this trilogy is bittersweet.

Special thanks to Michelle Awad, Jen Rogue, Kat Savage, Chris Rockwell, Amy Kay, and Kamelia Ani for providing poetry prompts and insight over the years that most definitely inspired and improved some of the poems in this book.

Stay Connected

Instagram: @thealiciacook
www.thealiciacook.com

Andrews McMeel Publishing
a division of Andrews McMeel Universal
1130 Walnut Street, Kansas City, Missouri 64106

www.andrewsmcmeel.com

23 24 25 26 27 MCN 10 9 8 7 6 5 4 3 2 1

ISBN: 978-1-5248-8620-2

Library of Congress Control Number: 2023942363

Editor: Patty Rice
Art Director/Designer: Julie Barnes
Production Editor: Meg Utz
Production Manager: Julie Skalla

ATTENTION: SCHOOLS AND BUSINESSES
Andrews McMeel books are available at quantity discounts with
bulk purchase for educational, business, or sales promotional use.
For information, please e-mail the Andrews McMeel Publishing
Special Sales Department: sales@amuniversal.com.